The Clue Books

INSECTS
and other small animals
without bony skeletons

GWEN ALLEN
JOAN DENSLOW

illustrations by
DEREK WHITELY

OXFORD
UNIVERSITY
PRESS

Oxford University Press, Walton Street, Oxford OX2 6DP

OXFORD NEW YORK TORONTO
DELHI BOMBAY CALCUTTA MADRAS KARACHI
PETALING JAYA SINGAPORE HONG KONG TOKYO
NAIROBI DAR ES SALAAM CAPE TOWN
MELBOURNE AUCKLAND

and associated companies in
BEIRUT BERLIN IBADAN NICOSIA

Oxford is a trade mark of Oxford University Press

PRINTED IN CHINA BY BRIGHT SUN (SHENZHEN) PRINTING LTD

FIRST PUBLISHED 1969
REPRINTED (with corrections) 1972, 1974, 1978, 1979,
1982, 1984, 1986

This book is about land animals without bony skeletons. There are many animals of this kind. They can be found under stones, in soil, among dead leaves, under the bark of trees, and on the leaves, flowers, and stems of plants.

In order to use this book you will need to look at real animals. A magnifying lens will help you to see them more clearly.

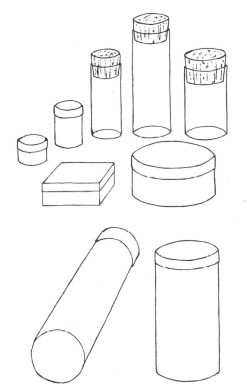

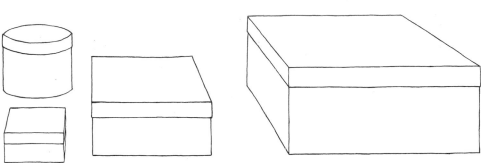

Small plastic boxes and tubes are useful for collecting the animals.

When you have looked at the animals, put them back where you found them; or if you wish to keep them for a short time look at pages 50–59 for instructions.

The real size of all the animals illustrated in this book is shown by a line ———— beside each drawing. When the line looks like this —→—— it means that the same kind of animal may be as small as this —→ or as large as this ————.

4 All animals without bony skeletons lay
eggs.

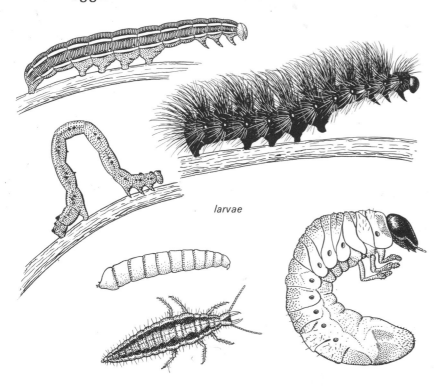

larvae

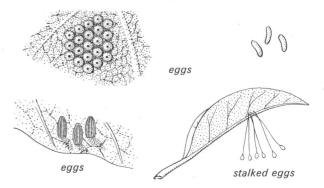

eggs

eggs

stalked eggs

Some eggs hatch into young animals that
do not at first look like their parents. At
this stage of their life they are called
LARVAE.

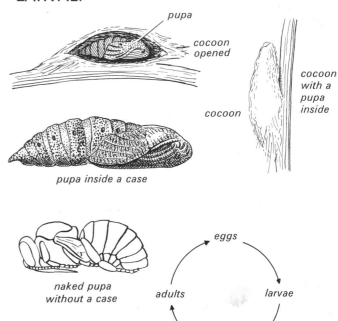

pupa

cocoon opened

cocoon with a pupa inside

cocoon

pupa inside a case

naked pupa without a case

eggs

larvae

pupae

adults

Each larva eats a great deal of food. It
sheds its skin every time the skin becomes
too small.

When the larva is full grown it changes
into a PUPA and later becomes an ADULT.

Some eggs hatch into young animals that look rather like their parents, except that they have no proper wings. These animals are called NYMPHS.

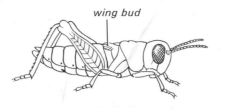

wing bud

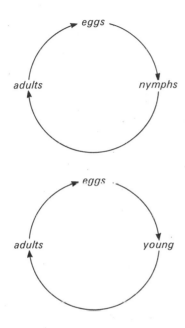

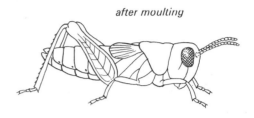

after moulting

Each nymph eats a great deal of food. It sheds its skin every time the skin gets too small for it.

After each moult the wings are seen to be bigger.

Some eggs hatch into young that look exactly like their parents, and some grow without shedding their skins.

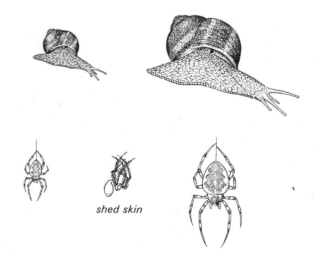

shed skin

When you have found an animal, the clues on pages 6–18 will help you to name it. Begin by using the clues on pages 6–7.

With a magnifying lens look carefully at the animal, find the clue that fits it, then turn to the page given for the next clue. Repeat this until you find its name or group.

CLUES TO NAMING LAND ANIMALS WITHOUT BONY SKELETONS
Most of the parts of animals drawn to illustrate the clues are larger than life size.

---

1. If it has wings, six jointed legs, and three parts to its body (head, thorax, and abdomen) it is an INSECT.

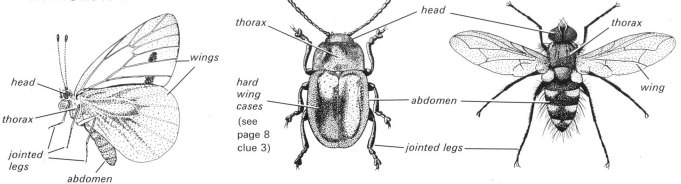

turn to page 8

---

2. If it has no wings, six jointed legs, and three parts to its body (head, thorax, and abdomen) it is an INSECT.

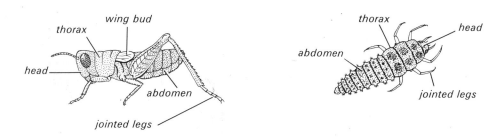

turn to page 14

3. If it has six jointed legs, some sucker feet, and no wings, it is a young insect called a CATERPILLAR.

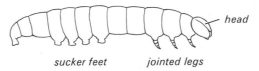

head

sucker feet   jointed legs

turn to page 15

4. If it has no wings, eight jointed legs, and only one or two parts to its body, it belongs to the SPIDER group.

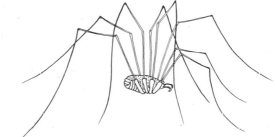

turn to page 16

5. If it has many jointed legs and no wings, it is a CENTIPEDE, MILLEPEDE, or WOODLOUSE.

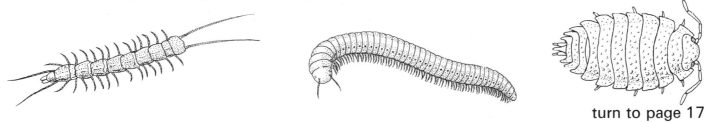

turn to page 17

6. If it has no legs and no wings

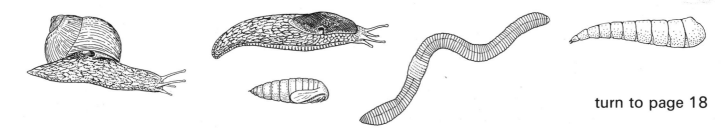

turn to page 18

From page 6, clue 1

Look carefully at the wings of the animal.

1. If the animal has two
   pairs of wings with
   POWDERY scales

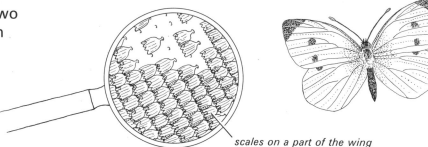

scales on a part of the wing

turn to page 9

2. If the animal has two pairs
   of transparent wings with
   veins

veins

turn to page 10

3. If the animal has two pairs of
   wings in which the upper
   wing forms a hard cover and
   the lower wings are
   transparent

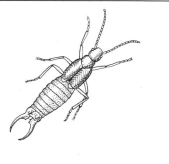

turn to page 12

4. If the animal has only one
   pair of wings

turn to page 13

Look carefully at its feelers. These are called antennae.

1. If the antennae have a club-shaped end, the animal is a BUTTERFLY.

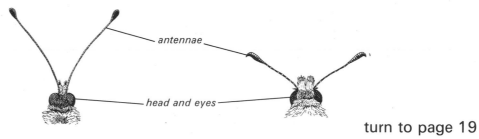

antennae

head and eyes

turn to page 19

2. If the antennae are without a club and look rather feathery,

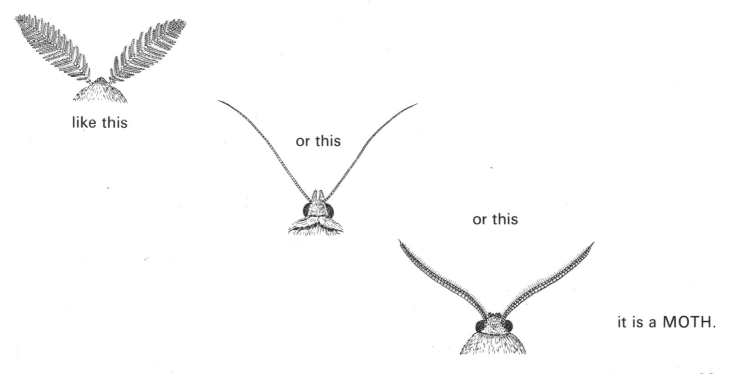

like this

or this

or this

it is a MOTH.

turn to page 22

From page 8, clue 2

Look carefully at the wings, the veins, and the size and shape of the abdomen (see page 6).

1. If the animal has wings
    with few veins and a short
    abdomen with a waist, it
    belongs to the BEE, WASP,
    and ANT group.

turn to pages 26, 28, 30

    If the animal has wings
    like this but no waist, it is
    a SAWFLY.

turn to page 30

---

2. If the animal has hairy wings
    with very few veins across
    them, the fore wings smaller
    than the hind ones, and a
    slender abdomen, it is a
    CADDIS-FLY.

turn to page 32

---

3. If the animal has hind wings
    very much smaller than the fore
    wings and rests with its
    wings upright, and if its
    abdomen has long tail
    filaments, it is a MAYFLY.

turn to page 32

4. If the animal has large wings with a complicated network of veins, small antennae, a large head, very large eyes, and a slender abdomen, it belongs to the DRAGONFLY family.

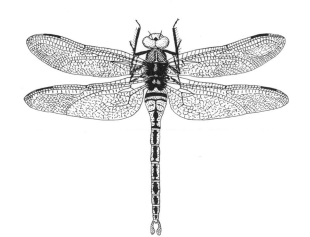

turn to page 32

5. If the animal is small and green, has delicate wings with a network of veins, and long antennae, it is a LACEWING.

   If it has dusky wings it is an ALDER-FLY.

turn to page 34

turn to page 32

6. If the animal is very small, green, black, yellowish, or brown, has wings with few veins, the hind wings smaller than the fore wings, has two points towards the end of its abdomen, and long antennae, it is an APHID (Green-flies, Black-flies, and others).

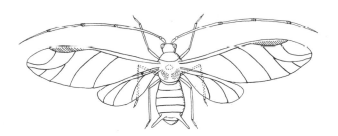

turn to page 34

From page 8, clue 3

Look carefully at the hard wing cases.

1. If the hard wing cases cover most of the body, the animal belongs to the BEETLE group.

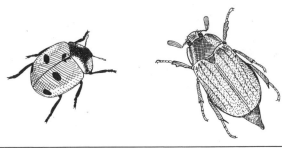

turn to page 36

2. If it has hard wing cases and a shield-like part (scutellum) on its back, the animal is a FROG-HOPPER or other BUG.

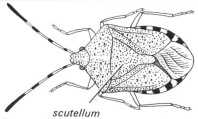

scutellum

turn to page 34

3. If the wings are longer than the horny cases, and the animal has very long hind legs, it belongs to the GRASSHOPPER group.

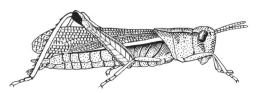

turn to page 40

4. If the hard wing cases cover the wings and are shorter than the body, and if the animal has a pair of pincers at the end of the abdomen, it is an EARWIG.

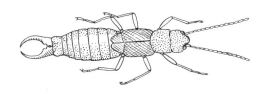

turn to page 40

5. If the hard wing cases are shorter than the body but there are no pincers, and if the animal rears its abdomen when disturbed, it is a DEVIL'S COACH-HORSE BEETLE or some other ROVE BEETLE.

see coloured illustration on page 39

From page 8, clue 4

This group of true flies with one pair of wings may be mistaken for bees or wasps.
If you use a magnifying lens you will see that there are always two small balancing organs,
called HALTERES, in place of hind wings.

1. If the animal has a body that is
almost as thick as it is long, often
covered with thick bristly hairs, it
belongs to the group of
SHORT-HORNED FLIES.

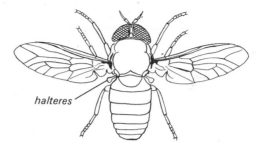

haltères

turn to page 42

2. If the animal has a humped
thorax, slender abdomen, and is
small, it belongs to the group of
MIDGES and MOSQUITOES
(Gnats).

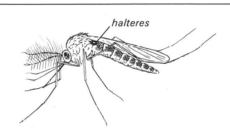

haltères

turn to page 42

3. If the animal has a humped
thorax, a slender abdomen,
long legs, and is large, it is a
CRANE-FLY (Daddy-long-legs).

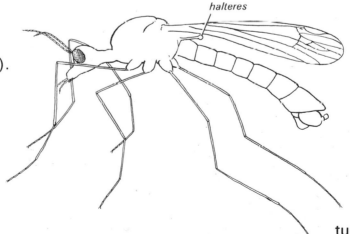

haltères

turn to page 42

From page 6, clue 2

1. If the animal has no sign of wings and an abdomen with a very small waist, it is an adult ANT.

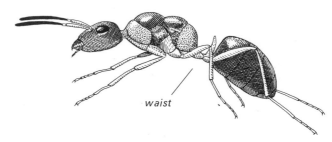

waist

turn to page 30

2. If the animal has no sign of wings, and if its abdomen has no waist, it is either an APHID

turn to page 34

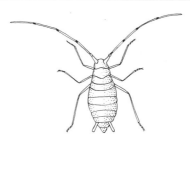

or a young insect called a LARVA.

turn to page 37

3. If the animal has small wing buds, it is a young insect called a NYMPH.

(Beware, an earwig's hard wing cases may be mistaken for wing buds; see page 8.)

turn to page 40

Using a magnifying glass, look carefully at the caterpillar's feet.

1. If the animal has five pairs of
   sucker feet, ALL with hooks,
   it is the LARVA of a
   BUTTERFLY or MOTH.

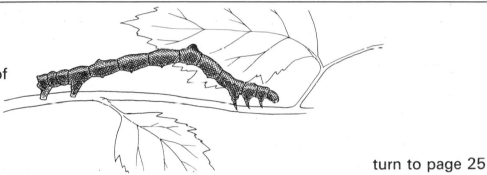

sucker feet

sucker foot

turn to pages 19–25

2. If the animal has only two
   pairs of sucker feet with
   hooks, it is a LOOPER
   CATERPILLAR, the larva of
   a MOTH.

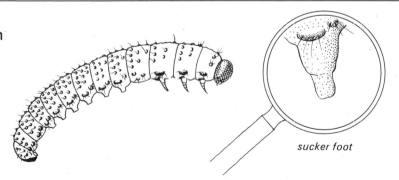

turn to page 25

3. If the animal has from six to
   eight pairs of sucker feet, with
   no hooks, it is a SAWFLY
   LARVA.

sucker foot

turn to page 30

From page 7, clue 4

Look carefully at the body of the animal.

1. If the animal has two parts to
   its body, with the legs
   attached to the front part, it is
   a SPIDER.

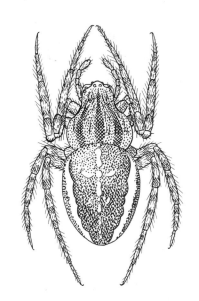

turn to page 44

2. If the animal has only one
   part to its body it may be
   either a HARVESTMAN,
   if it has very long legs or,
   a MITE if it is very small.

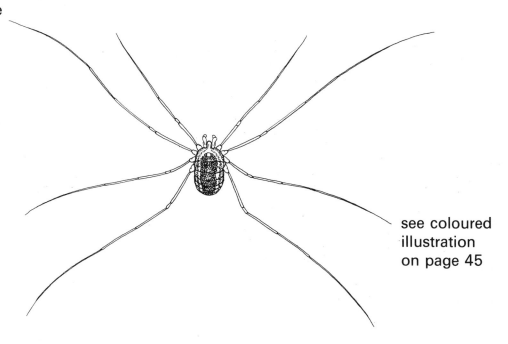

see coloured
illustration
on page 45

1. If the animal has an oval-shaped body with less than fifteen rings, called SEGMENTS, and appears to have similar legs on most of them, it is a WOODLOUSE.

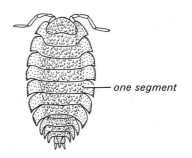

one segment

turn to page 46

2. If the animal has a long slender body with more than fifteen segments, and has one pair of long jointed legs on each segment of its body, it is a CENTIPEDE.

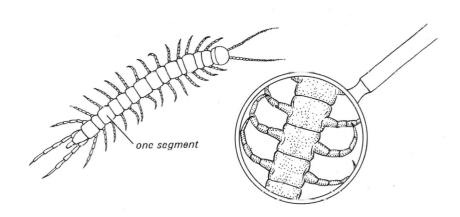

one segment

turn to page 46

3. If the animal has a long slender body with more than fifteen segments, and has two pairs of small jointed legs on each segment of its body, it is a MILLEPEDE.

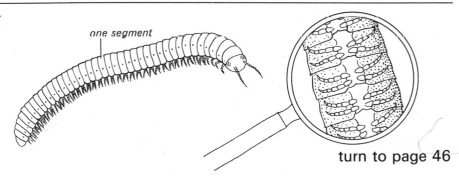

one segment

turn to page 46

From page 7, clue 6

1. If the animal has a shell, two
    pairs of tentacles, and a
    slimy foot, it is a
    SNAIL.

foot

turn to page 48

2. If the animal has no shell,
    two pairs of tentacles, and a
    flat slimy foot, it is a
    SLUG.

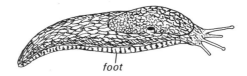
foot

turn to page 48

3. If the animal has no shell,
    and the body is made up of
    thirteen or fewer rings, called
    segments, it is an insect
    LARVA (see page 4).

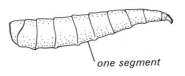
one segment

turn to pages
26, 28, 30, 42

4. If the animal has no shell,
    and the body is made up of
    more than 100 rings, called
    segments, it is an
    EARTHWORM.

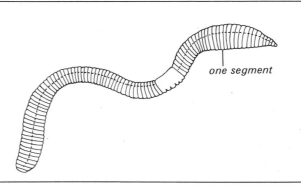
one segment

turn to page 46

5. If the animal is not like any
    of these, it is probably an
    insect pupa.

    Keep your pupa in a box with damp peat to see what it turns into.

turn to page 4

From page 9, clue 1, and page 15, clue 1

BUTTERFLIES may be seen in spring and summer. The butterfly feeds on nectar which it sucks from flowers, using the proboscis (a long tube) which is coiled up like a spring beneath its head when not in use. Most butterflies lay their eggs on the plants that the caterpillars will feed on when they hatch (see page 4).

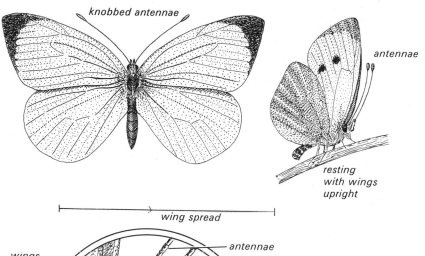

knobbed antennae

antennae

resting with wings upright

wing spread

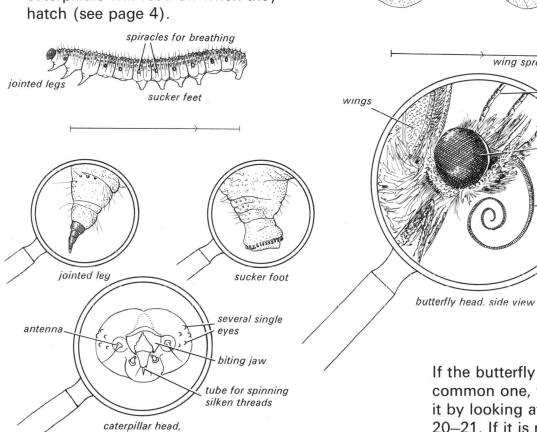

spiracles for breathing

jointed legs

sucker feet

jointed leg

sucker foot

antenna

several single eyes

biting jaw

tube for spinning silken threads

caterpillar head, front view

wings

antennae

compound eye made of many single eyes

coiled proboscis

butterfly head, side view

If the butterfly you have found is a common one, you will be able to name it by looking at the illustrations on pages 20–21. If it is more rare you will need to look at a butterfly book.

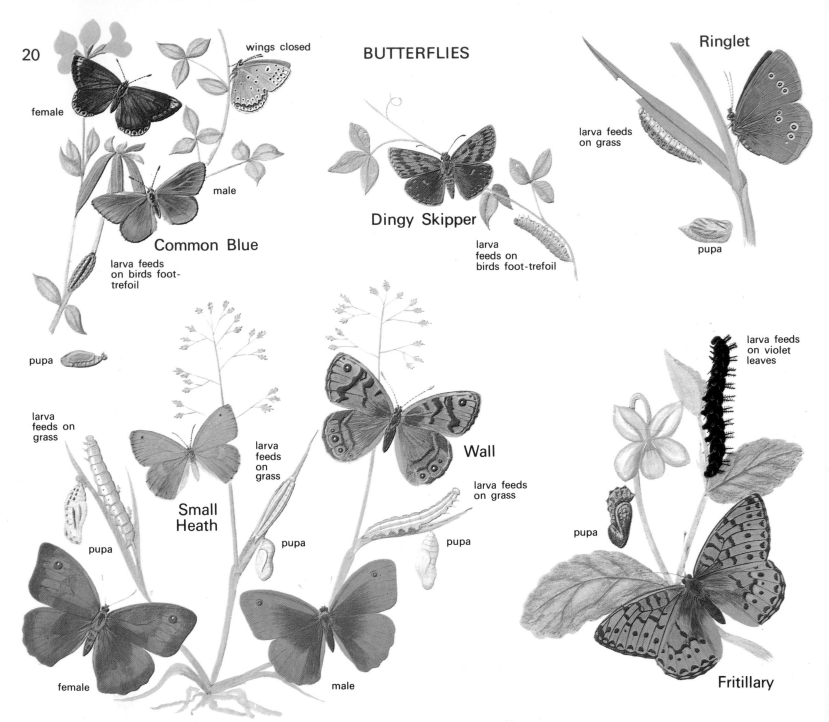

20

BUTTERFLIES

Ringlet

wings closed

larva feeds
on grass

female

pupa

larva feeds
on grass

male

Common Blue

Dingy Skipper

larva feeds
on birds foot-
trefoil

larva
feeds on
birds foot-trefoil

pupa

larva feeds
on violet
leaves

larva
feeds on
grass

Wall

larva
feeds
on
grass

larva feeds
on grass

Small
Heath

pupa

pupa

pupa

pupa

female

male

Fritillary

Meadow Brown

larva feeds on
stinging nettles

Small Tortoiseshell

pupa

pupa

larva feeds on
stinging nettles

Small White

Green Veined
White

larva feeds
on cabbage
or nasturtium

pupa

Red Admiral

larva feeds on
garlic mustard
or water cress

pupa

male

pupa

Large White

pupa

female

Brimstone

larva feeds
on cabbage

larva feeds on
buckthorn

male

female

From page 9, clue 2, and page 15, clue 1

MOTHS may be seen from spring until the frosts
come in autumn. Some of them feed on nectar
which they gather from night-scented
flowers. Most moths fly at night and rest
with their wings spread. They lay their
eggs on the plants that the caterpillars will
eat when they hatch
(see page 4).

resting

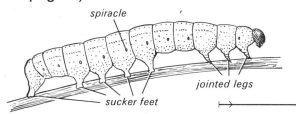

spiracle

jointed legs

sucker feet

wing spread

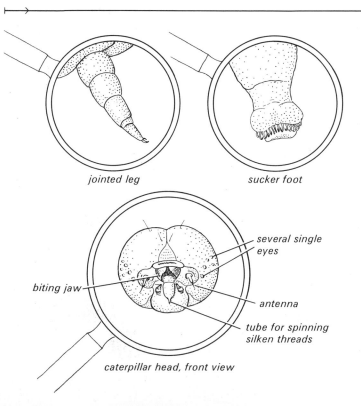

jointed leg

sucker foot

several single eyes

biting jaw

antenna

tube for spinning silken threads

caterpillar head, front view

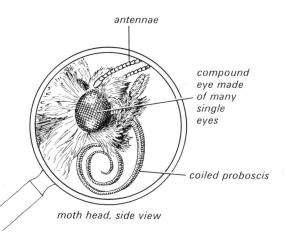

antennae

compound eye made of many single eyes

coiled proboscis

moth head, side view

If the moth you have found is a
common one, you may be able to name
it, or its group, by looking at the
illustrations on pages 23–25. As there
are hundreds of different kinds of
moths you may need to look in a moth
book.

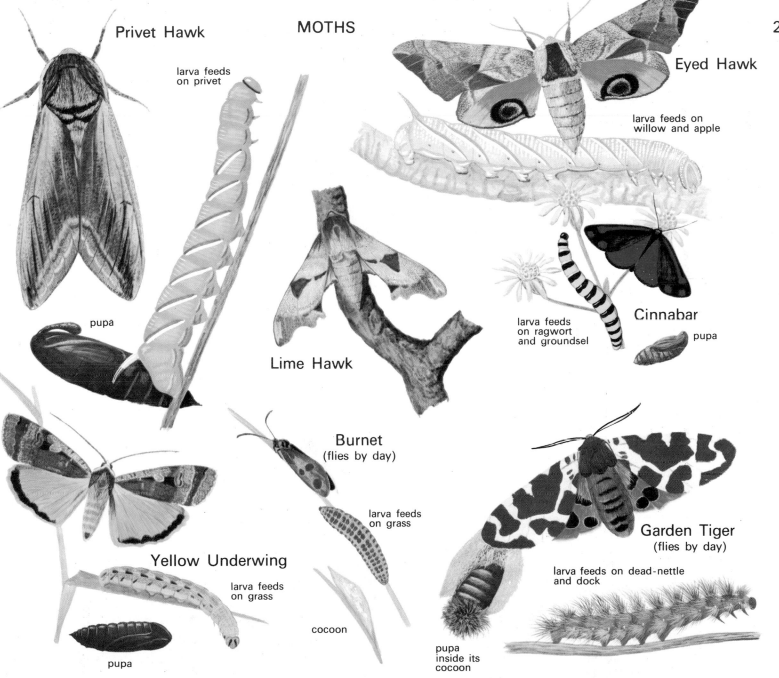

Privet Hawk

larva feeds
on privet

pupa

Eyed Hawk

larva feeds on
willow and apple

Lime Hawk

Cinnabar

larva feeds
on ragwort
and groundsel

pupa

Yellow Underwing

larva feeds
on grass

pupa

Burnet
(flies by day)

larva feeds
on grass

cocoon

Garden Tiger
(flies by day)

larva feeds on dead-nettle
and dock

pupa
inside its
cocoon

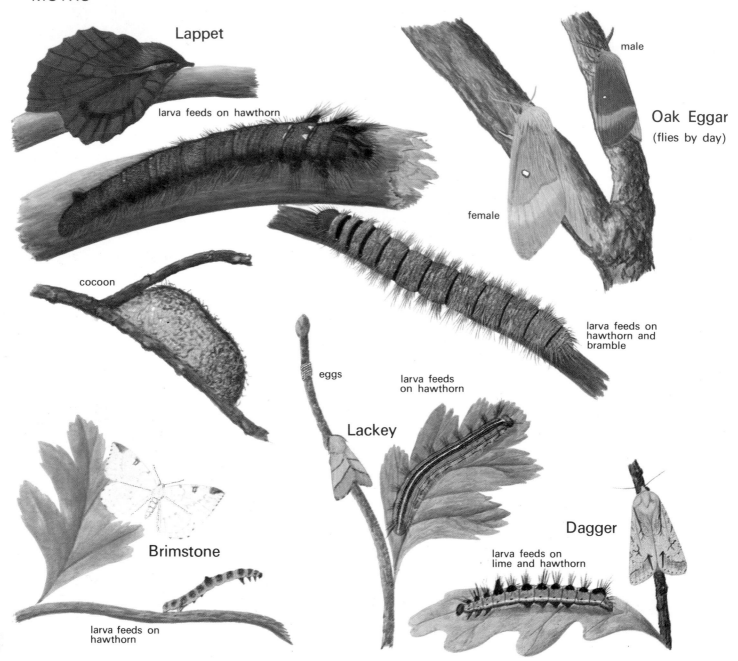

Lappet

larva feeds on hawthorn

Oak Eggar
(flies by day)

male

female

larva feeds on
hawthorn and
bramble

cocoon

eggs

larva feeds
on hawthorn

Lackey

Brimstone

larva feeds on
hawthorn

Dagger

larva feeds on
lime and hawthorn

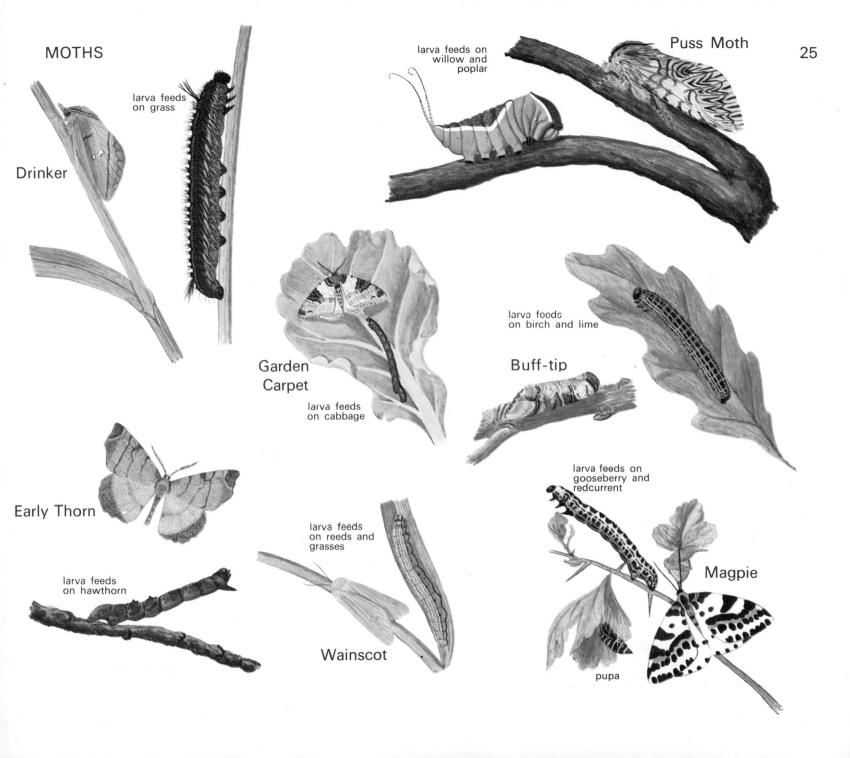

MOTHS

larva feeds on willow and poplar

Puss Moth

larva feeds on grass

Drinker

larva feeds on birch and lime

Buff-tip

Garden Carpet

larva feeds on cabbage

larva feeds on gooseberry and redcurrent

Early Thorn

larva feeds on hawthorn

larva feeds on reeds and grasses

Wainscot

Magpie

pupa

From page 10, clue 1, and page 18, clue 3

BEES

HONEY BEES. The worker bees may be seen from early spring until late autumn gathering nectar and pollen from flowers on sunny days. They use their long hollow tube, called a proboscis, to collect the nectar. The pollen clings to their hairy bodies and they use their front and hind legs to brush it into the pollen baskets (see illustrations below).

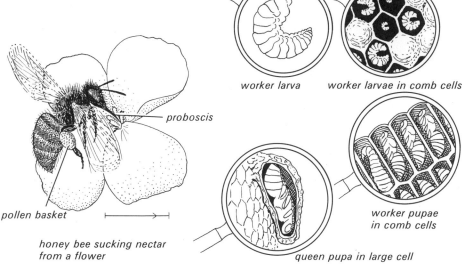

proboscis

pollen basket

honey bee sucking nectar from a flower

worker larva

worker larvae in comb cells

worker pupae in comb cells

queen pupa in large cell

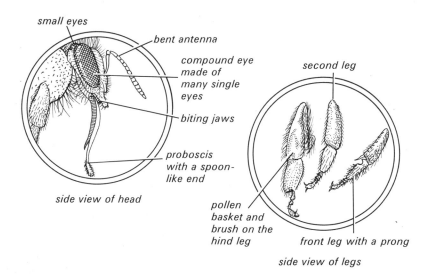

small eyes

bent antenna

compound eye made of many single eyes

biting jaws

proboscis with a spoon-like end

side view of head

second leg

pollen basket and brush on the hind leg

front leg with a prong

side view of legs

You can see the proboscis and pollen baskets quite clearly by watching bees visiting flowers on warm, sunny days. Honey bees live in hollow trees and in hives provided by beekeepers. They make combs of six-sided cells with wax, which they scrape from glands underneath their abdomens. Honey is stored and eggs are laid by the queen in different parts of the comb. During the winter the workers and queens live in the hive feeding on the stored honey.

BUMBLE BEES make themselves small nests in the ground and sleep during the winter.

There are many different kinds of bees. If there is no picture on page 27 of the one you have found, you will need to look at a book about bees.

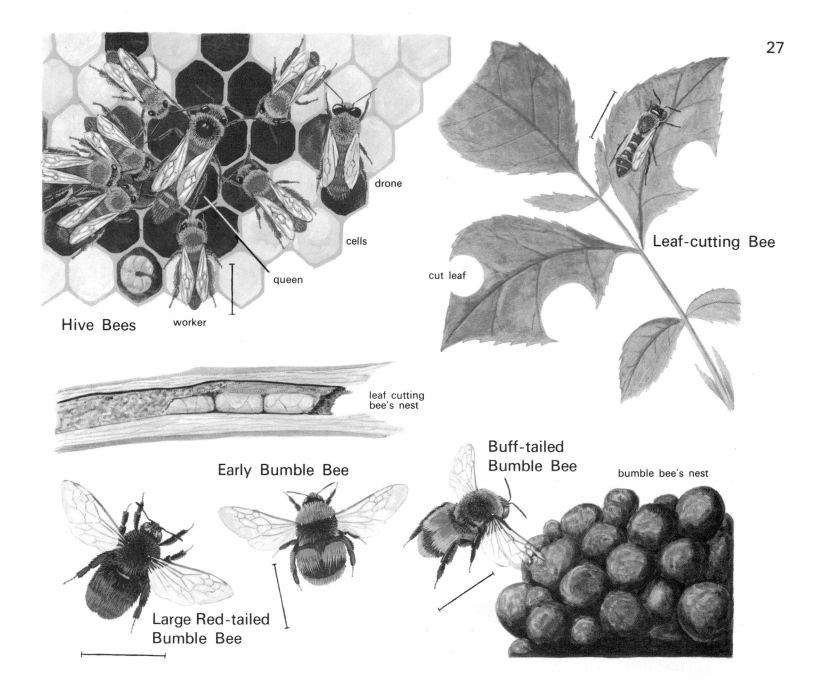

Hive Bees

drone

cells

queen

worker

Leaf-cutting Bee

cut leaf

leaf cutting bee's nest

Early Bumble Bee

Buff-tailed Bumble Bee

bumble bee's nest

Large Red-tailed Bumble Bee

From page 10, clue 1, and page 18, clue 3

WASPS

The queen wasp comes out of hibernation in early spring and begins to build the first cells of the nest. She lays an egg in each of these cells. When the eggs hatch she catches insects to feed the larvae (see life cycle on page 5). In a short time the larvae become pupae and then worker wasps.

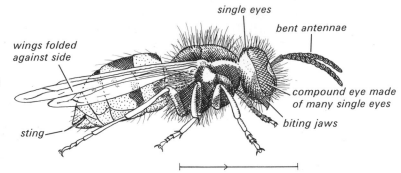

single eyes

bent antennae

wings folded against side

compound eye made of many single eyes

sting

biting jaws

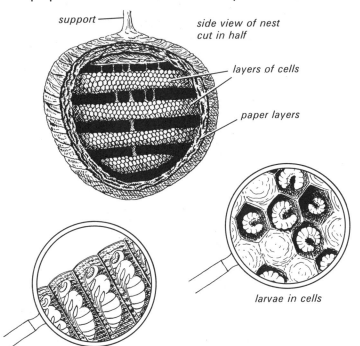

support

side view of nest cut in half

layers of cells

paper layers

larvae in cells

pupae in cells

In summer worker wasps scrape wood to make paper to enlarge the nest; they collect food for new larvae.

The queen continues to lay eggs but takes no further part in nest building or the care of the young. Wasps feed mainly on fruit and other sweet things. In autumn when the frosts come all wasps, except the queen, die.

SOLITARY WASPS live alone and the females make small nests. Digger wasps build them in holes in the ground. Potter wasps often hang them from plants. The female lays one egg in each cell. She catches and paralyses insects or small animals, which she puts into the cells for the larvae to feed on.

ICHNEUMON AND CHALCIS FLIES

Ichneumon flies lay eggs in insects, particularly caterpillars, on which their larvae feed. When the larvae are full-grown they become pupae; then the insect they have been feeding on dies.

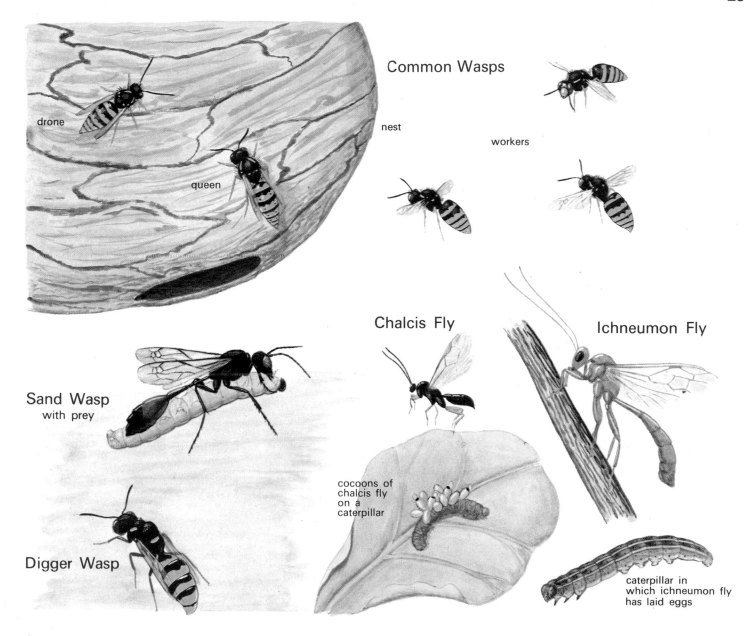

Common Wasps

drone

queen

nest

workers

Sand Wasp
with prey

Digger Wasp

Chalcis Fly

Ichneumon Fly

cocoons of
chalcis fly
on a
caterpillar

caterpillar in
which ichneumon fly
has laid eggs

30   From page 10, clue 1, page 14, clue 1, and page 15, clue 3

ANTS

Ants live all the year round in the soil of gardens, meadows and woodlands. The queen begins to lay eggs in early spring (see life cycle, page 5). Groups of eggs, larvae, and pupae are cared for by worker ants. In late summer on hot sultry days, small winged males and large winged queens fly from the nests in swarms. After mating, the queen returns to the nest and bites off her wings. Ants feed mainly on sweet juices from fruits and from green-flies. They make tracks from the nest, which they follow when foraging.

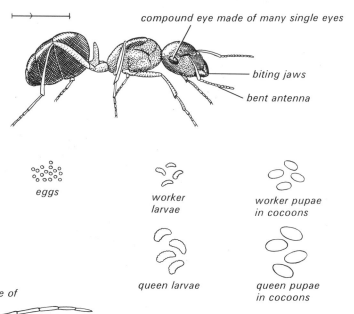

compound eye made of many single eyes

biting jaws

bent antenna

eggs

worker larvae

worker pupae in cocoons

queen larvae

queen pupae in cocoons

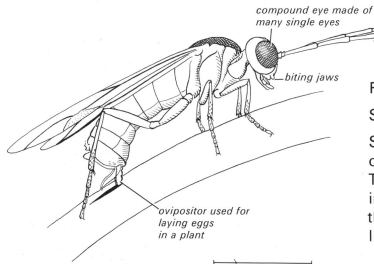

compound eye made of many single eyes

antennae

biting jaws

ovipositor used for laying eggs in a plant

From page 15, clue 3

SAWFLIES

Sawflies have a saw-like tube called an ovipositor through which they lay their eggs. These they lay in minute holes that they saw in the stems or leaves of the plants on which the caterpillars will feed when they hatch (see life cycle, page 5).

Red Ants

31

male   queen   worker

mound   worker

Black Ants

queen   male

mound

worker

Hawthorn Sawfly

Apple Sawfly

larva

Gooseberry
Sawfly

worker   male   queen

Wood Ants

larva

pupa

larva

pupa

larva

cocoon

32　The animals shown on this page lay their eggs in water.
As the young live in water they are not shown in this
book about land animals.

From page 11, clue 4

DRAGONFLIES

Dragonflies dart about near
water, catching flying insects.
They hold the insects between
their legs while feeding on
them.

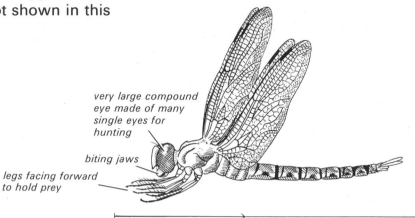

very large compound
eye made of many
single eyes for
hunting

biting jaws

legs facing forward
to hold prey

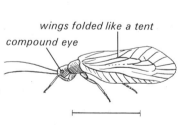

compound eye

very small jaws

From page 10, clue 3

MAYFLIES

Swarms of mayflies dance over the water
surface on warm sunny days.
The last skin is shed after their first flight.
Before this moult fishermen call them
'duns'; afterwards they call them
'spinners'. Adult mayflies live for only a short
time because they cannot feed.

From page 11, clue 5

ALDER-FLIES

Alder-flies may be seen
resting among plants by
streams.

wings folded like a tent
compound eye

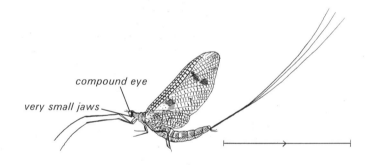

hairy wings   long slender antennae
compound eye

small jaws
used for
licking juices

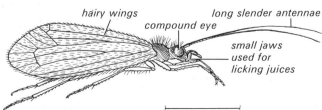

From page 10, clue 2

CADDIS-FLIES

Caddis-flies often rest among plants during
the day, and usually fly at night. They lick up
sweet juices.

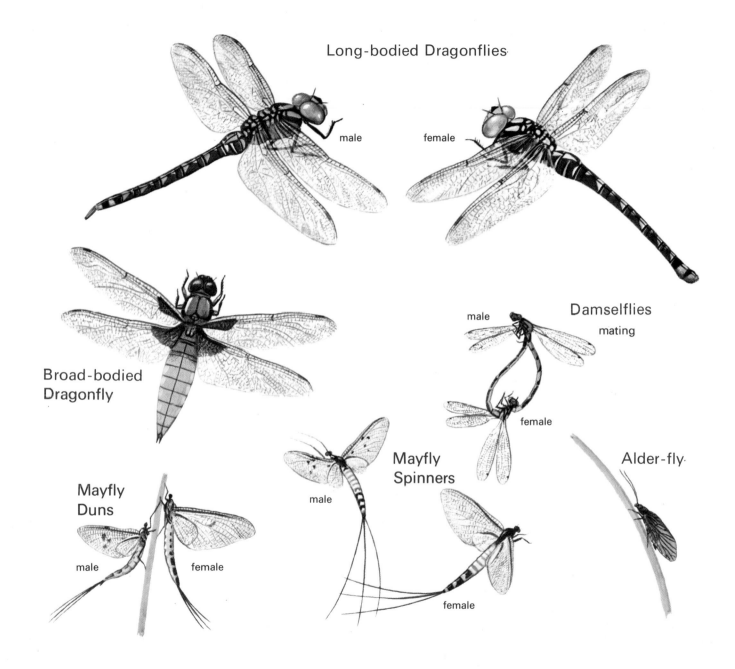

Long-bodied Dragonflies

male

female

Broad-bodied
Dragonfly

Damselflies

male

mating

female

Mayfly
Spinners

male

female

Alder-fly

Mayfly
Duns

male

female

Mayfly
Spinners

male

female

From page 11, clue 5

LACEWINGS

Lacewings live in gardens during the summer.
They lay clusters of stalked eggs on the top of
plants on which aphids feed. Both the larvae and
the adult lacewings feed on aphids.

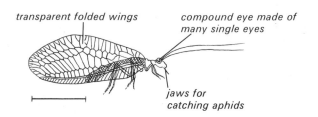

transparent folded wings *compound eye made of many single eyes*

jaws for catching aphids

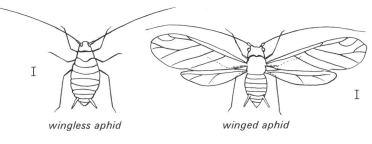

wingless aphid *winged aphid*

From page 11, clue 6, and page 14, clue 2

APHIDS

Aphids may be black, green or white. They
pierce plants with their sharp jaws and suck
up the juices. Aphids breed very rapidly.
Hundreds of them of different ages and sizes
may be seen on plants. Most of the aphids are
wingless; but the winged ones fly to new
food plants and start new colonies.

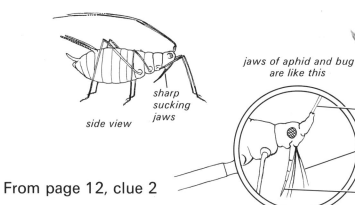

side view

sharp sucking jaws

jaws of aphid and bug are like this

antenna

sharp piercing jaws

sucking tube

From page 12, clue 2

BUGS

Shieldbugs, capsid bugs and frog-hoppers are
the more common bugs. During the summer
adults and nymphs (see life cycle, page 5) suck
juices from plants. Frog-hoppers live in long
grass, and hop when disturbed. The nymphs may
be found during June inside 'cuckoo-spit', a
froth-like substance which the nymphs make by
mixing air with the juices of plants as they pass
through their bodies.

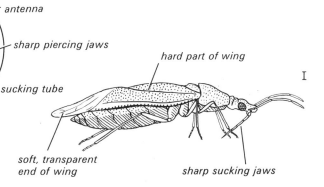

hard part of wing

soft, transparent end of wing

sharp sucking jaws

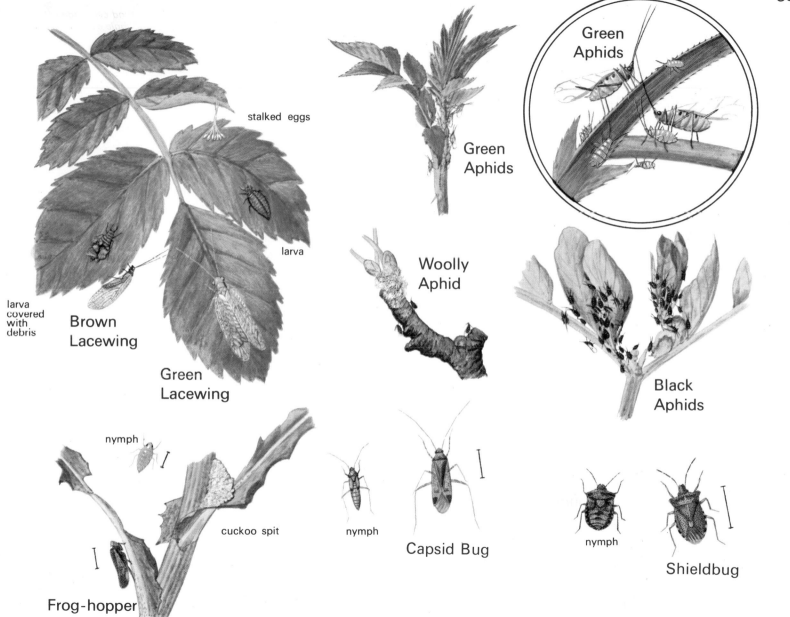

stalked eggs

larva

larva covered with debris

Brown Lacewing

Green Lacewing

Green Aphids

Green Aphids

Woolly Aphid

Black Aphids

nymph

cuckoo spit

Frog-hopper

nymph

Capsid Bug

nymph

Shieldbug

From page 12, clue 1

BEETLES

Beetles may be found almost anywhere but more especially under stones and among plants. All beetles have biting jaws; some feed on live animals; some on plants; and others, the scavengers, feed on dead plants and animals.

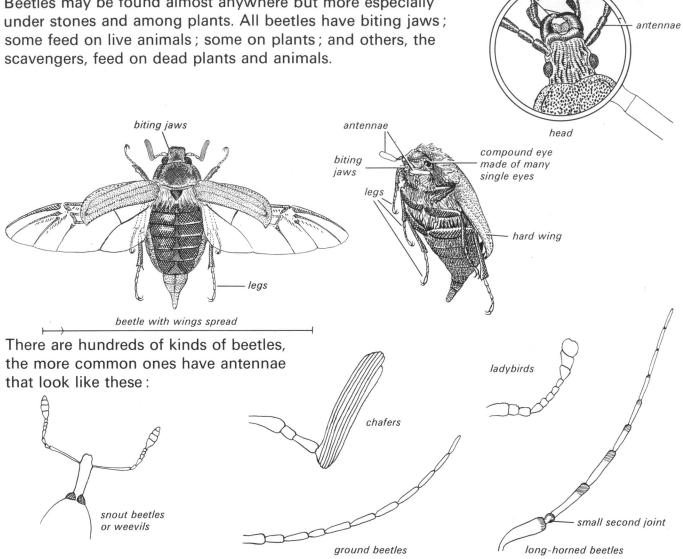

biting jaws

antennae

head

biting jaws

antennae

biting jaws

compound eye made of many single eyes

legs

hard wing

legs

beetle with wings spread

There are hundreds of kinds of beetles, the more common ones have antennae that look like these:

ladybirds

chafers

snout beetles or weevils

ground beetles

small second joint

long-horned beetles

(all are enlarged)

All beetles lay eggs where the larvae will find food when they hatch. Some larvae hunt for
their food ; some are fat and soft bodied and feed on rotten wood or roots.
The larvae usually turn into pupae underground and so do not need to be protected by a hard
covering.

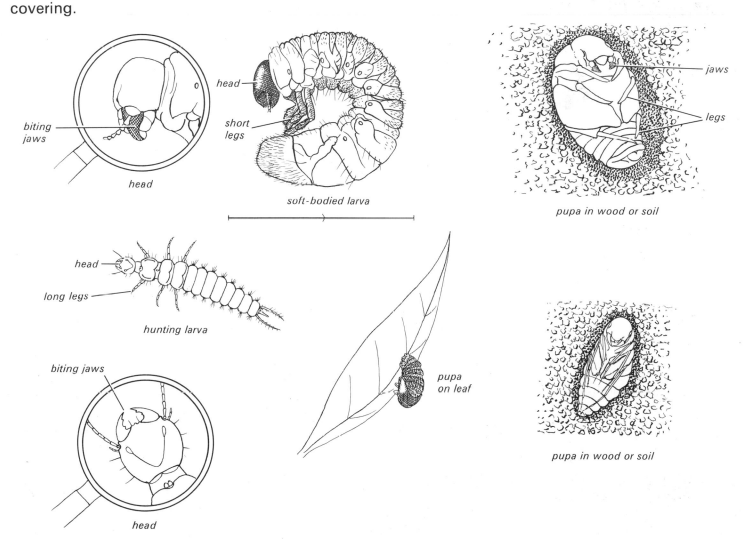

biting
jaws

head

head

short
legs

soft-bodied larva

jaws

legs

pupa in wood or soil

head

long legs

hunting larva

biting jaws

head

pupa
on leaf

pupa in wood or soil

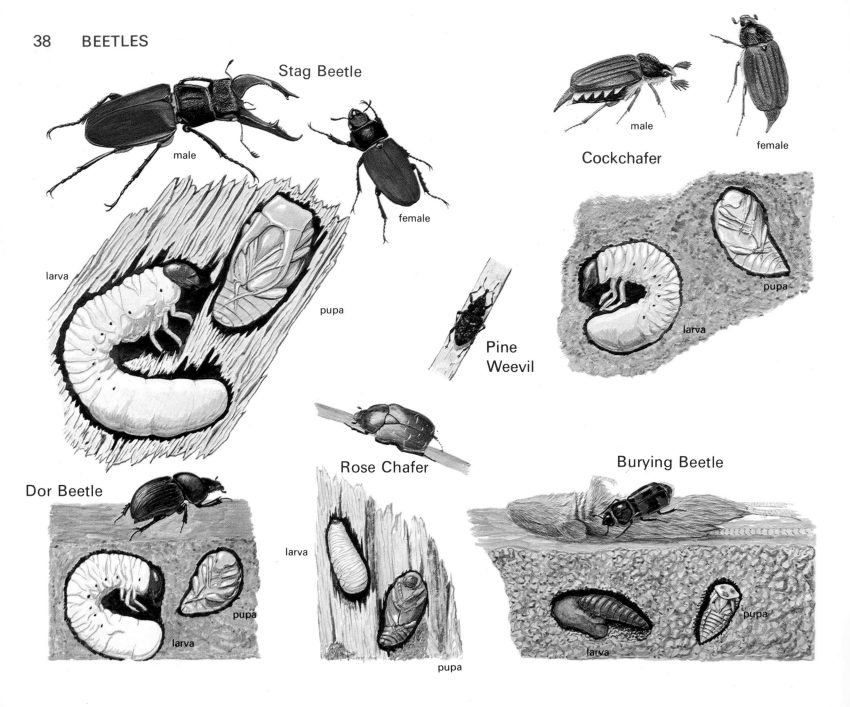

Stag Beetle

male

female

larva

pupa

Cockchafer

male

female

larva

pupa

Pine
Weevil

Dor Beetle

larva

pupa

Rose Chafer

larva

pupa

Burying Beetle

larva

pupa

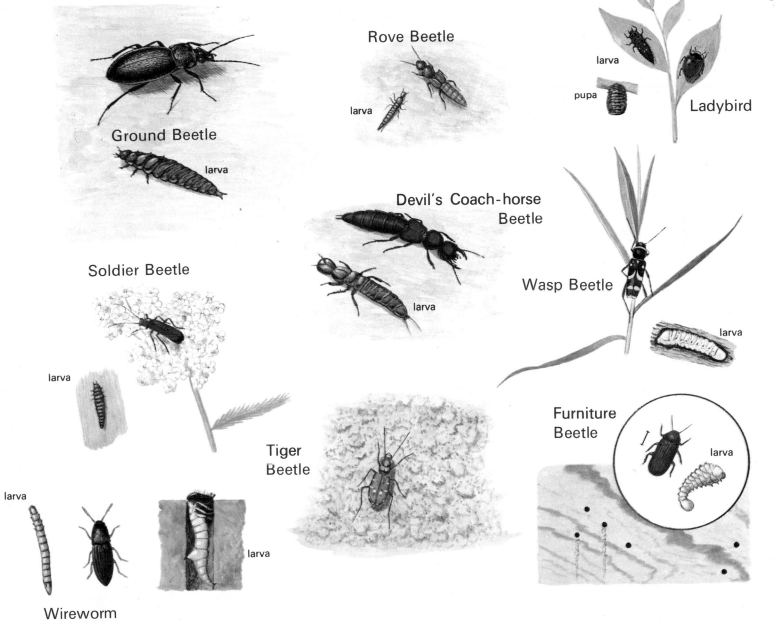

39

Ground Beetle

larva

Rove Beetle

larva

Ladybird

larva

pupa

Devil's Coach-horse
Beetle

larva

Soldier Beetle

larva

Wasp Beetle

larva

Tiger
Beetle

Furniture
Beetle

larva

larva

larva

Wireworm

From page 12, clue 3, and page 14, clue 3

GRASSHOPPERS AND CRICKETS

Grasshoppers live among plants, in hedgerows, in long grass, and on heathland. They may be heard chirruping on warm sunny days. They make the sound by rubbing their hind legs against the outside edge of their wings. They have very long hind legs and are able to jump long distances. Most grasshoppers feed on plants though the Great Green Grasshopper sometimes eats animals.

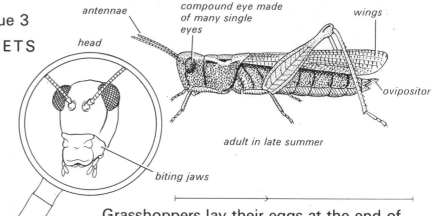

antennae

head

compound eye made of many single eyes

wings

ovipositor

biting jaws

adult in late summer

Grasshoppers lay their eggs at the end of the summer in a hole in the ground which they make with their ovipositor (the tube through which the eggs are laid) ; then they die. The eggs do not hatch until the following spring.

Crickets are very like grasshoppers but come out at night. House Crickets live in or near buildings.

The Great Green Grasshoppers and crickets make their chirruping noise by rubbing their wings together.

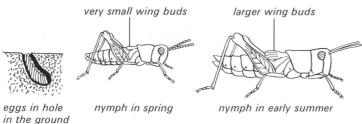

very small wing buds

larger wing buds

eggs in hole in the ground

nymph in spring

nymph in early summer

From page 12, clue 4, and page 14, clue 3

EARWIGS

Earwigs may be found in flowers, rotten wood, under stones, and in other damp dark places. They nibble flower petals but are mainly scavengers (page 36). The female earwig lays eggs in a small hole in the ground or in rotten wood, and then guards them until the nymphs that hatch are old enough to look after themselves.

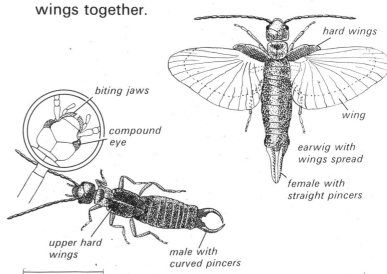

biting jaws

compound eye

hard wings

wing

earwig with wings spread

female with straight pincers

upper hard wings

male with curved pincers

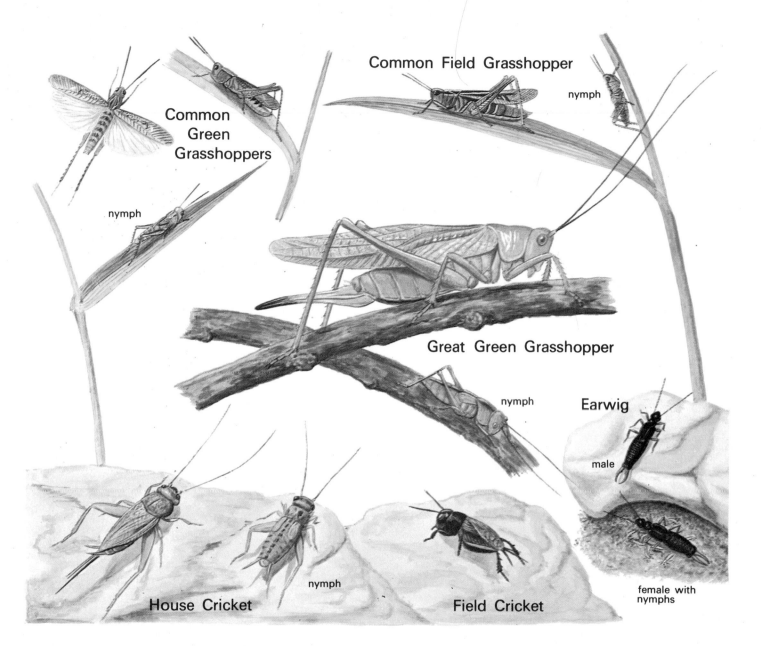

Common Green Grasshoppers

nymph

Common Field Grasshopper

nymph

Great Green Grasshopper

nymph

Earwig

male

female with nymphs

House Cricket

nymph

Field Cricket

From page 13, clues 1, 2, and 3, and page 18, clue 3

FLIES

Flies suck up juices from decaying plants and animals or nectar from flowers. Midges and mosquitos may suck blood as well. Many hover-flies may be seen on sunny days hovering over flowers or darting from one to the other.

Many flies lay their eggs on the dead plants or animals which the larvae (maggots) will eat when they hatch.

Hover-fly larvae feed on aphids (see page 34). Crane-flies lay their eggs in grass; the larvae (leather-jackets) eat the roots.

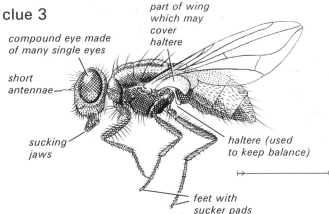

part of wing which may cover haltere

compound eye made of many single eyes

short antennae

sucking jaws

haltere (used to keep balance)

feet with sucker pads

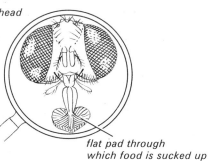

head

flat pad through which food is sucked up

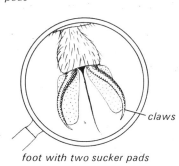

claws

foot with two sucker pads

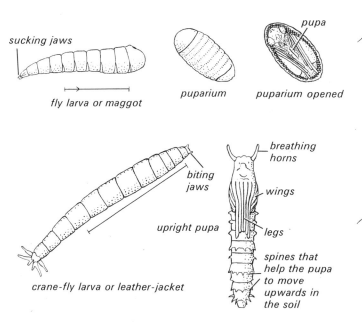

sucking jaws

fly larva or maggot

pupa

puparium

puparium opened

breathing horns

biting jaws

wings

upright pupa

legs

spines that help the pupa to move upwards in the soil

crane-fly larva or leather-jacket

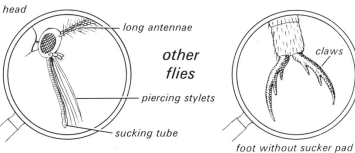

head

long antennae

other flies

piercing stylets

sucking tube

claws

foot without sucker pad

Midges and mosquitoes lay their eggs in water; as the larvae and pupae live in water they are not shown in this book about land animals.

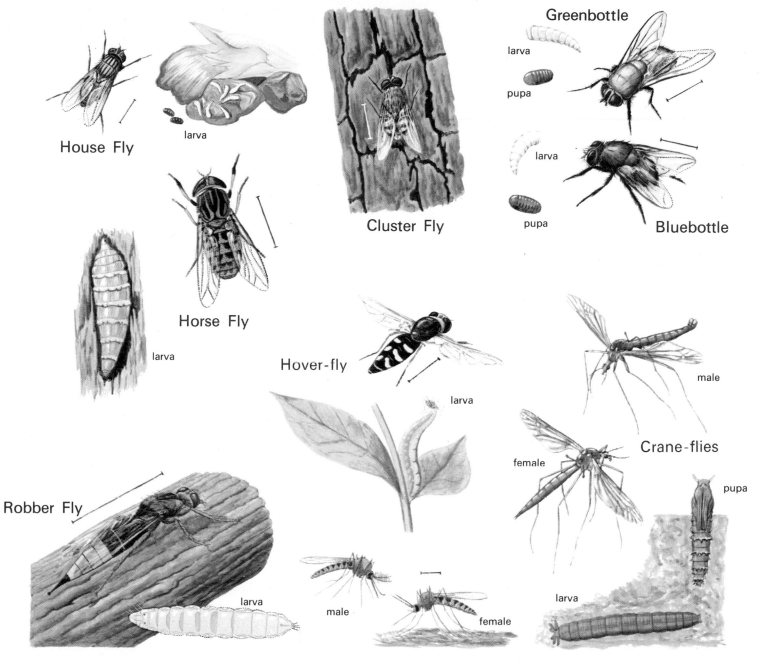

43

House Fly

larva

Cluster Fly

Greenbottle

larva

pupa

larva

pupa

Bluebottle

Horse Fly

larva

Hover-fly

larva

male

Crane-flies

female

pupa

Robber Fly

larva

larva

male

female

Mosquito (Gnat)

larva

From page 16, clue 1

44

SPIDERS

Spiders live in buildings, cracks in walls, and among plants. They all spin silk and always use a thread as a lifeline when they move from one place to another.

Many spiders use their silk for making webs to catch animals for food. Different groups of spiders have their own particular web shapes (see p. 45). When the webs become damaged they have to be mended or remade.

Hunting spiders chase their prey; because they need to see clearly, two of their eyes are very large.

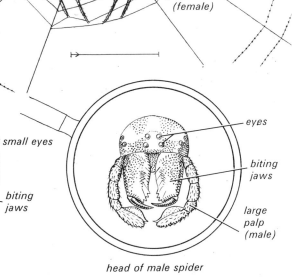

spider seen from below hanging on a web

spinnerets for spinning silk

hind legs used when clinging

biting jaws

palps (female)

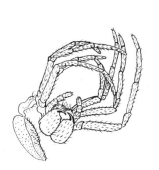

shed spider skin (see p. 56)

large eyes

small eyes

biting jaws

head of hunting spider

eyes

biting jaws

large palp (male)

head of male spider

untidy cocoon of eggs camouflaged by dust mixed with silk

tidy cocoon of eggs

Spiders lay eggs and wrap them up in silk to form a cocoon. They hatch into tiny spiders (see life cycle, page 5).

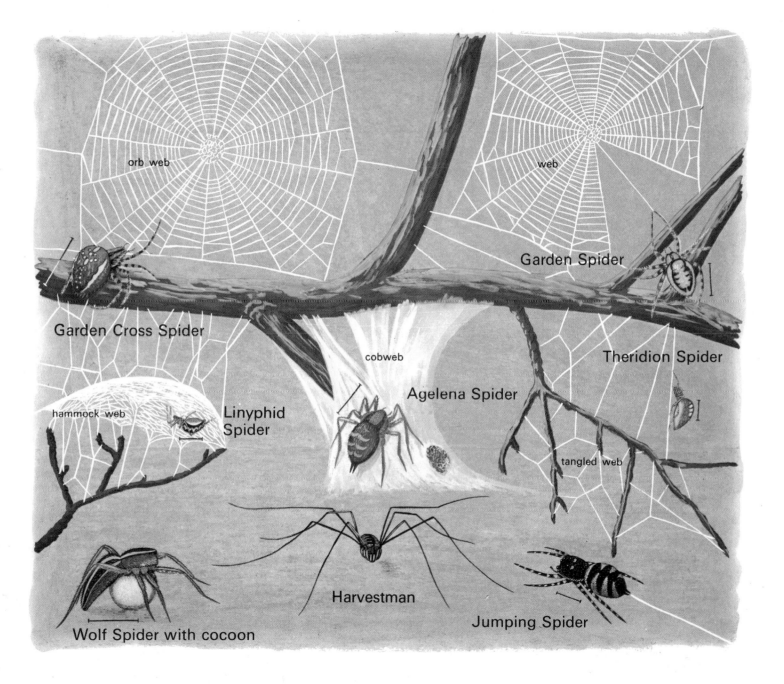

orb web

web

Garden Spider

Garden Cross Spider

Theridion Spider

cobweb

Agelena Spider

hammock web

Linyphid
Spider

tangled web

Harvestman

Wolf Spider with cocoon

Jumping Spider

From page 17, clue 1

WOODLICE

Woodlice live under stones and in rotten logs. When frightened some kinds roll themselves up into a ball.

The females carry their eggs and young under their bodies. The young are like their parents and shed their skins as they grow.

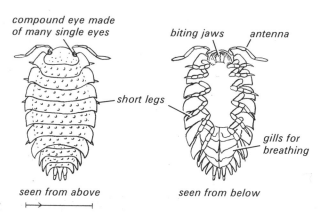

compound eye made of many single eyes

biting jaws   antenna

short legs

gills for breathing

seen from above

seen from below

From page 17, clue 2

CENTIPEDES

Centipedes are fierce hunting animals. They live in damp, dark places and lay their eggs in the soil. These hatch into young like their parents (see life cycle, page 5).

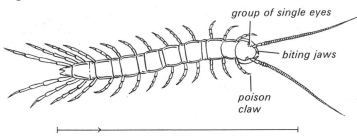

group of single eyes

biting jaws

poison claw

From page 17, clue 3

MILLEPEDES

Millepedes nibble plants and are garden pests. They live in damp soil and lay their eggs in small nests of soil. When the young hatch, they have only a very few legs; these grow later and more appear after each moult.

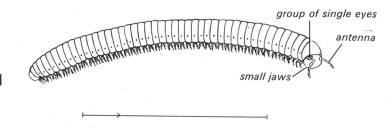

group of single eyes

antenna

small jaws

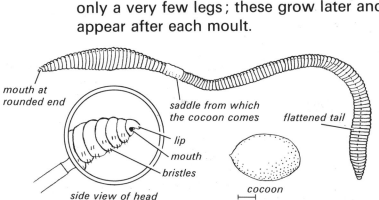

mouth at rounded end

saddle from which the cocoon comes

flattened tail

lip

mouth

bristles

side view of head

cocoon

From page 18, clue 4

EARTHWORMS

Earthworms live in burrows which they make by pushing and eating the soil away. Some kinds make worm casts from the soil they have eaten; they also pull leaves down into their burrows. They lay eggs in cocoons; these hatch into minute worms like their parents (see life cycle, page 5).

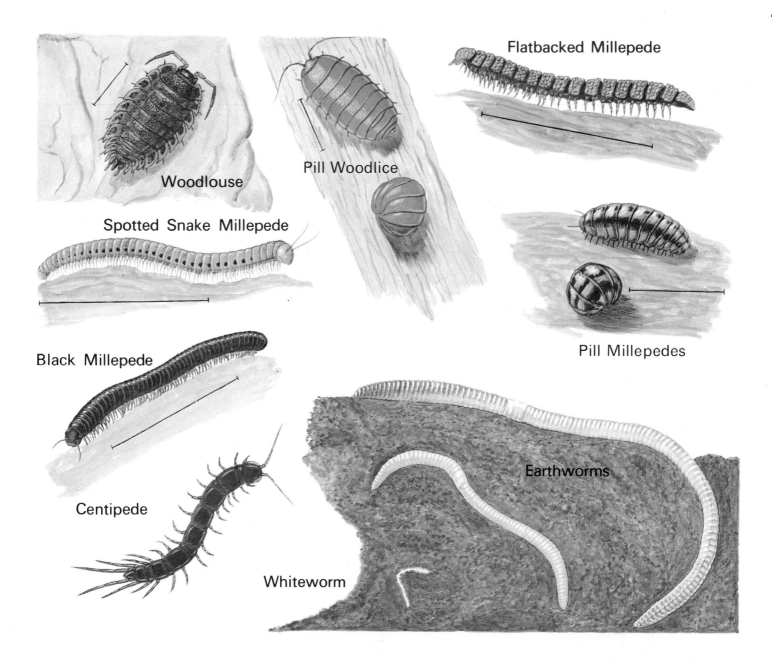

Woodlouse

Pill Woodlice

Flatbacked Millepede

Spotted Snake Millepede

Pill Millepedes

Black Millepede

Centipede

Earthworms

Whiteworm

From page 18, clues 1 and 2

SNAILS AND SLUGS

Snails and slugs live among plants,
under stones, or in the soil; they move
about when it is damp. The slime trail
from the slime gland helps them to cling
as they move along using their muscular
foot (see page 58).

They chew plants with their long
tongues that are covered with hundreds
of teeth.

Snails seal themselves in their shells
when the weather is very dry or cold.

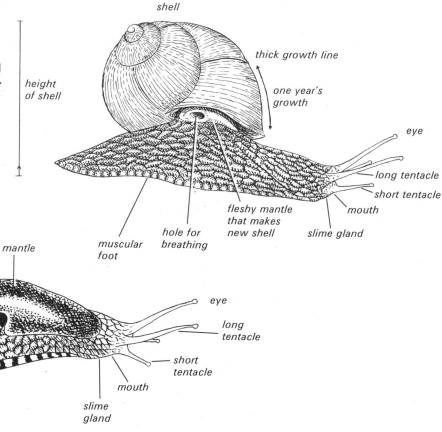

They both lay eggs in the soil which
hatch into tiny animals like their parents
(see life cycle, page 5).
The shell of the snail gets bigger as the
snail grows.

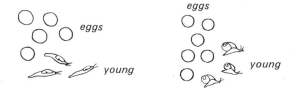

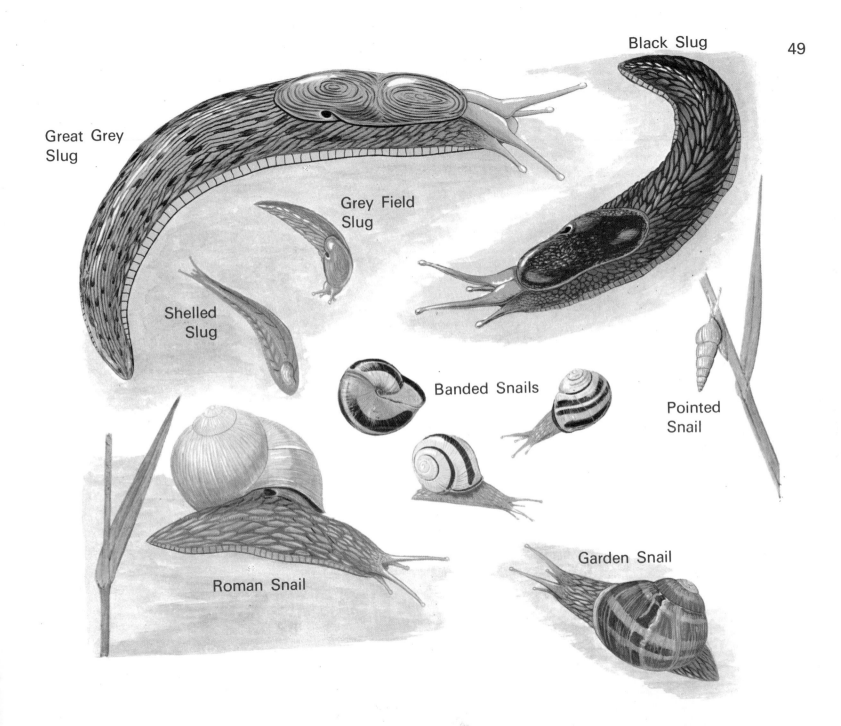

Black Slug

Great Grey
Slug

Grey Field
Slug

Shelled
Slug

Banded Snails

Pointed
Snail

Roman Snail

Garden Snail

The illustrations on pages 50 and 51 will give you ideas for different kinds of homes that animals without bony skeletons will need if they are to be kept in captivity.

The vivaria illustrated are made in large glass jars, but glass tanks or clear plastic boxes are also suitable. Vivaria may also be made as shown on page 51, number 5.

2. VIVARIUM FOR ANTS AND WORMS

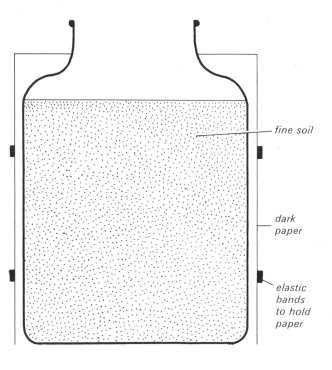

fine soil

dark paper

elastic bands to hold paper

1. VIVARIUM FOR CATERPILLARS

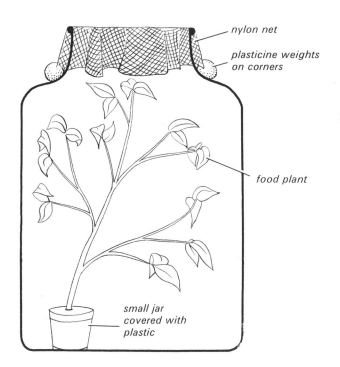

nylon net

plasticine weights on corners

food plant

small jar covered with plastic

Pages 51–59 tell you how to care for and study the animals you keep in homes like these.

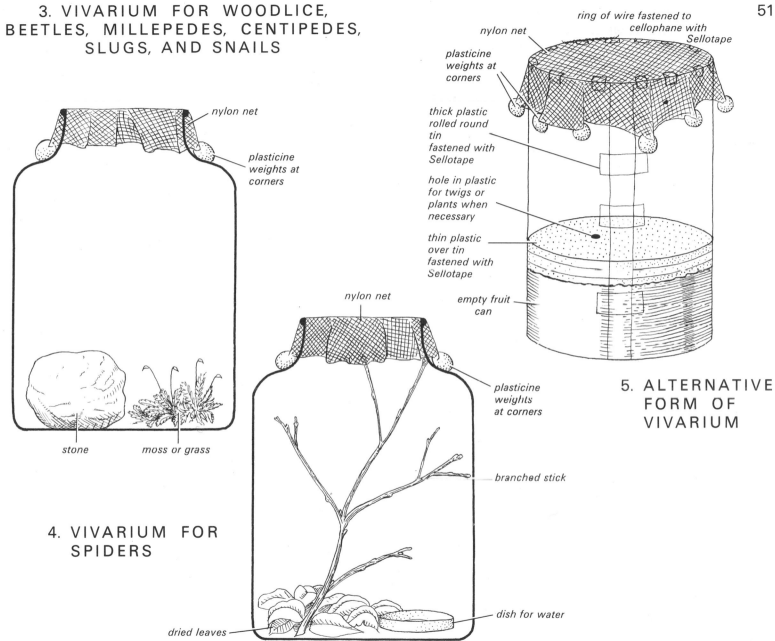

3. VIVARIUM FOR WOODLICE, BEETLES, MILLEPEDES, CENTIPEDES, SLUGS, AND SNAILS

nylon net

plasticine weights at corners

stone

moss or grass

4. VIVARIUM FOR SPIDERS

nylon net

plasticine weights at corners

branched stick

dried leaves

dish for water

ring of wire fastened to cellophane with Sellotape

nylon net

plasticine weights at corners

thick plastic rolled round tin fastened with Sellotape

hole in plastic for twigs or plants when necessary

thin plastic over tin fastened with Sellotape

empty fruit can

5. ALTERNATIVE FORM OF VIVARIUM

When collecting caterpillars it is essential to pick some of the plant on which they are feeding, as they will probably only eat that kind of plant. Look at pages 20, 21, 23–5 for pictures of caterpillars on their food plants.

Eggs, caterpillars, and pupae may be bought from Butterfly Farms. The farms will supply catalogues that tell you which food plants are required for each kind of caterpillar.

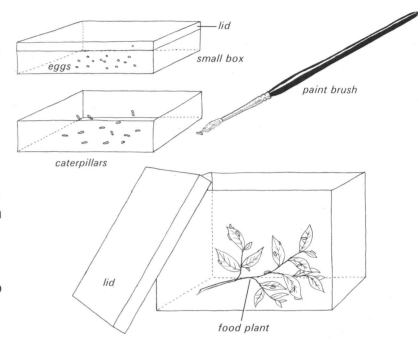

All eggs should be kept in a small plastic box WITHOUT LEAVES with the lid closed until they hatch. When the caterpillars are a few hours old, they should be moved into a box containing the correct food plant. A soft paint brush will be needed to move them without damaging them. The lid should be kept on the box for some days to prevent them from getting too dry.

When they are about half an inch long, the caterpillars may be put into a vivarium, page 50. The vivarium will need to be cleaned each day and the leaves changed because the caterpillars get their water from the leaves: they do not drink.

To learn more about how caterpillars behave watch them closely.

Find out *what plants they eat, how they eat, how they move, when and how they rest,
when and how they shed their skins, when and how they pupate,
what happens when you touch them gently with a paint brush.*

Keep a record of how your caterpillar behaves. This is one way of keeping records:

name of caterpillar

date it was found

where it was found

what plant it was feeding on

date	what you saw it doing	when it shed its skin	when it pupated	when the pupa hatched

If you find or buy eggs, you will need to add the date of hatching.

Two ways of showing the approximate amount of leaf eaten each day.

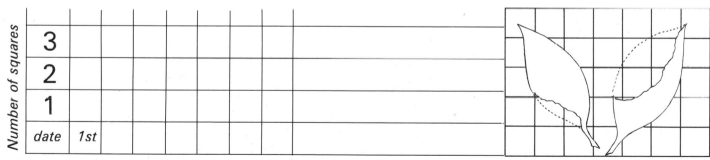

You can also keep a record of how much your caterpillar grows each day.

In order to keep these records you will need to keep each caterpillar in a separate vivarium.

If you wish to keep ants, look for an ants' nest (see page 30). In June and July the nests usually contain many larvae and pupae as well as workers and queens; earlier in the year you may find the tiny eggs as well. Dig up the nest with as many larvae, pupae, and adult ants as you can, and put it into a large tin or bucket. If there are any large lumps of soil, break them up before you tip your collection into the vivarium (see page 50). The ants will not escape if they are well kept.

soil and ants' nest

trowel

stones thrown away

Keep the soil moist by putting a teaspoonful of water along the top of the soil each day. Feed the ants on sugar and green-fly; put some wet sugar on cotton wool in a small cup made of kitchen foil, and sink it in the soil at the top of the vivarium. Pick a small piece of plant with green-fly on it and put it on top of the soil.

The dark paper may be removed for a short time so that you may watch what the ants are doing.

After watching the ants for some time you should be able to answer these questions:

Ants usually keep larvae and pupae of different ages and sizes in different groups.

How many groups have your ants?   How often do the ants move them around?

In what ways have you seen the ants using their antennae?

Ants often carry loads as big as themselves.

What have you seen your ants carrying?   How do they carry things?
What other things have you seen the ants doing?

Beetles and centipedes are difficult to keep in captivity, but they may be kept for a few days if you want to watch how they move and what they do. Most beetles and centipedes eat small animals, though they may feed on small pieces of raw meat; if they are given raw meat it must be removed after an hour or two if it is not eaten.

After a few days the beetles or centipedes should be returned to the place where they were found or one similar.

Woodlice and millepedes feed on plants and may therefore be kept in captivity for a longer time. Give them some rotten wood, leaves, and small pieces of different kinds of fruit and vegetables. Stale food will need to be removed and fresh given each day.

Try to find out: *what they eat*

what you think they like best

when they eat

when they move about

when they rest

Ladybird beetles may often be found in spring in pairs; if you keep them in a vivarium similar to the one for caterpillars (see page 50), and feed them on fresh green-fly daily, they will probably lay eggs (see life cycle on pages 4 and 39). The larvae will need to be fed on green-fly.

House spiders and garden spiders are particularly interesting to keep in captivity (see page 51). If you are keeping a hunting spider, you will need moss or a tuft of grass instead of dried leaves.

All spiders need live food and will eat each other if more than one is put in each vivarium. A live house fly or bluebottle should be put into each vivarium once a week.

When flies are plentiful, spiders eat many of them to make fat to store in their bodies; this fat is used as food during the winter when flies are scarce.

Look out for remains of food on the webs of garden and house spiders to find out what different kinds of food the spiders have eaten.

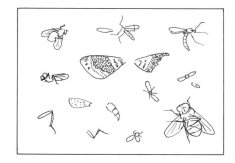

As spiders grow they moult a number of times, and it is often possible to find the skins of house spiders in their webs. You may be able to find a series of skins from the very young spider $\frac{1}{4}$ inch or so long to the large spider with legs $1\frac{1}{2}$ inches long.

Mount them in a shallow box and cover them with cellophane.

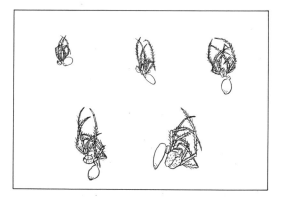

Catch a garden spider on a stick.

Shake it gently from the end of the stick; you will see that it will fasten its silken thread to the stick before it falls.

How far does it fall?

Watch it climb back to the stick.

Which legs does it use?

What does it do with the silken thread?

Look in the corners and crannies of sheds, fences, and walls and among bushes for spiders' webs.
You may like to keep a record of your findings like this:

date	wheel web where found	date	cobweb where found	date	hammock web where found	date	tangled web where found
Oct. 2 3 4	corner of window web was broken new web in the same corner	Sept. 25	corner of shed by flower pot	Aug.	in garden hedge		

When you have kept a record for some months, you will have found out
which is the most common web in your area
what time of the year the webs are built most frequently
where the webs are most often built

If you watch young spiders escaping from their cocoons, you will see that they use their silken threads as parachutes. This is the gossamer thread that you feel on your faces when you walk along in the morning in spring and summer.

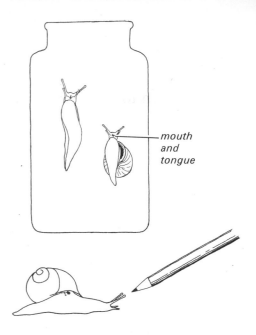

mouth and tongue

Slugs and snails are easy to keep in captivity, but they will escape unless a piece of glass or perforated zinc is put across the top of the vivarium. They need fresh leaves every day. Give them different kinds of leaves to find out which they like best.

Watch the slugs and snails climbing up the glass sides of the vivarium; you will see their foot muscles rippling and the trail of slime being left behind. If a snail refuses to come out of its shell, put it in a saucer with a little slightly warm water.

To find out how well a snail can see, move a pencil or a stick carefully near its eyes (see page 48). How near can you get before the snail pulls in its tentacles?

Look for slugs and snails out of doors after rain or at night when the air is damp.

You may like to keep records of your findings like this:

| date | number of | | temperature | whether wet or dry | whether windy or still |
	slugs	snails			

When you have kept these records for some time, you will know what conditions slugs and snails prefer.

Look under stones and plants in dry summer weather or in winter to find snails that have sealed themselves inside their shells (see page 48).

Mark some snails by putting a small spot of enamel paint on their shells.

Either put them back where you found them and collect them every now and again to see how far they travel.

Or having marked them, move them a short distance from where you found them and see how long it takes them to get home again.

If you wish to keep worms in captivity you will need to fill the vivarium with damp soil (see page 50) or with alternate layers of fine soil and sand.

Then find two or three fairly large worms from the garden or compost heap and put them on the top of the soil. Watch them to see how long they take to bury themselves.

When you are not watching them you must remember to put the black paper round the jar, or the worms will not come near the glass.

Each day you will need to scatter a teaspoonful of water over the soil in the vivarium.

Some worms pull leaves, very small pieces of carrot, apple, and other things into their tunnels. Find out if yours do so by putting some pieces on top of the soil and looking the next day to see if the worms have moved them.

> *What things do they seem to like best?*
> *Which leaves do they like best?*

If you listen to a worm crawling over a piece of paper you will hear the scratching of the bristles (see page 46).

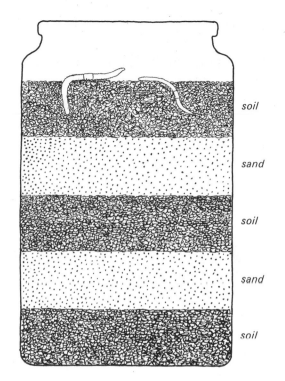

soil

sand

soil

sand

soil

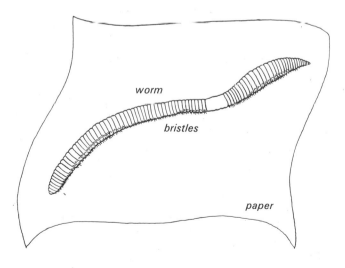

worm

bristles

paper

Bibliography

Burton, John, *The Oxford Book of Insects* (Oxford University Press)
Butterflies of Wayside and Woodland, compiled Stokoe from R. South (Warne)
Haworth, F. M., *Garden Creatures* (Univ. London Press)
Haworth, F. M., *Wasps* (Univ. London Press)
Janus, H., *The Young Specialist Looks at Molluscs* (Burke)
Linssen, E. F., and Newman, L. H., *Observer Book of Common Insects and Spiders* (Warne)
Observer Book of Butterflies, compiled Stokoe from R. South (Warne)
Warnecke, G., *The Young Specialist Looks at Butterflies and Moths* (Burke)

Index